PRIMO

Ed Davidson

Primo is copyright © 2017 by Edward Davidson

All rights reserved. No part of this publication may be reproduced, distributed, or transmitted in any form or by any means, electronic or mechanical, including photocopying, recording, or other electronic or mechanical methods, or by any information storage and retrieval system, without the prior written permission of the author.

Professionals and amateurs are hereby warned that this material is fully protected under the Copyright Laws of the United States of America and all other countries of the Berne and Universal Copyright Conventions. All rights including, but not limited to, professional, amateur, recording, motion picture, recitation, lecturing, public reading, radio and television broadcasting, and the rights of translation into foreign languages are expressly reserved. Particular emphasis is placed on the question of readings and all uses of this book by educational institutions.

www.primostageplay.com

ISBN: 978-0-9987096-4-2

Cover photo of Primo Levi: © Jillian Edelstein

Cover and interior design: Doug Williamson
Editors: Mary DeDanan
       Melanie Graysmith
Printed by Minuteman Press of Berkeley, California

First Edition: November 2017

DEDICATED

To those individuals who wake up each morning wanting to express the essence of their life's journey artistically: for their time— from their place— through their eyes. This passion to create comes from within. We are wired differently than others, not better, not more important, just different. Whatever path we choose to express ourselves, it is done with a singular belief: having something to say to the world. Only a few reach the stratosphere of influence, fame, and fortune, while the rest struggle meaningfully in oblivion as part of the continuum.

I entered the Holocaust from a world of sunshine and freedom, untouched by war and its horrors. Living an everyday existence that most of us experience: gliding through the days cherishing the joys, problem-solving the sorrows, while accepting the simple plainness of life. Striving to comprehend the annihilation, I traveled into the darkness of the human soul, seeking meaning through Auschwitz's lens, ultimately ending in the silent stillness of the empty ramp, where those who "walked on" confronted me with haunting eyes.

Ed Davidson

INTRODUCTION

THE STORY

In 1987, Primo Levi, the Italian writer renowned for his autobiographical *Survival in Auschwitz*, his novels, and other writings about the Holocaust, died after falling down the stairwell of his apartment house. This play is a fictional account of Levi's last day. In it, Levi questions the relevance of his writings to the new generation while journeying into the dreamscape of his memory to a day in Auschwitz.

Primo's aim is defining Auschwitz to the emerging generations.

Written as a screenplay, it was adapted for stage readings, and then developed into a stage play. Transitioning to the stage was problematic: *Primo* has fifty characters, more than thirty scenes, and a strong visual interpretation of the storyline with rapid scene changes. Changing any of these elements would destroy the work as it was conceived and written. The only option was to create a new, unique way of staging a theatrical production.

Primo projects a very different interpretation of movement, rhythm, and pace in a stage play. It is more akin to a movie on stage, yet it relies entirely on the power of live performance, building on the actors' ability to convey the storyline through the experiences of the characters. Fusing the power that the actors bring to the performance with the successful integration of all the other elements in the production creates a chemistry encapsulating *Primo*'s essence that transcends the boundaries of the stage. This transports the audience into an imaginary world, disrupting the viewers' complacency by awakening their inner spirits.

THE STAGING

Choreographic Movement
Dialogue alone cannot portray Auschwitz. Choreographic movement, similar to dance but different in structure, is essential in creating the reality of the concentration camp's environment, while displaying its emotional and debilitating impact. Created without music, working in conjunction with the dialogue or separately on its own, this movement is an integral part in depicting the camp experience that brings a visual intensity and fluidity to the realism of the performance. It brings another dimension to the piece, similar to a painter unlocking the potential of a canvas's two-dimensional surface by invigorating the flatness with the power of perspective, creating a third dimension.

A choreographer will create a visual narrative from segments of the action, through movement or mime, and then integrate that narrative with the other elements of the scene to move the story forward. Choreographic movement is not used in every scene, but is present throughout the work.

Bending Time
The present is experienced through Levi's eyes as he moves through the day unaware of his impending fate. Simultaneously, the past is perceived through the dreamscape of his memory, reconstructing the world of the concentration camp. Each step forward draws him further into his memories, blurring the distinction between past and present as their boundaries vanish. He moves into the mist of timelessness, drifting through its shadows and currents, sensing the faint whisperings of distant voices as they beckon. The play emerges as a timeless depiction of Auschwitz driven by the prisoner's experience, defined by the survivor's memory.

Ensemble
There are twelve actors playing fifty characters. They are sup-

ported by eighteen dancers who perform the visual aspects of the story, either separately or in conjunction with the actors. Most of the characters only appear once or in a few scenes, while a small number appear throughout the play.

In the present, each character is dressed differently according to the part they are playing. In the past, every character is wearing a uniform, making it difficult for the audience to separate and recognize individual prisoners from the nameless, shapeless bodies moving around the stage. The only way they can be identified is by recognizing their particular situation. Each situation represents a unique problem which defines the prisoner, setting him apart from the others until his dilemma is resolved (usually requiring several scenes). The challenge confronting the actor is defining the predicament their character experiences while maintaining their individuality, through the turbulence of their plight. In most situations the protagonist interacts with the same prisoners and frequents recurring locations, enhancing the viewer's ability to follow each situation to its conclusion.

Even though the prisoners seem identical, they represent two distinct groups: the veterans who have been in camp long enough to understand how the system works, and the Hungarian prisoners who have just arrived, confused and in shock. The disparity between these two groups brings them into conflict while, individually, each prisoner struggles to endure the constant perils of the camp.

Every situation develops chronologically. All situations flow to the camp's rhythm, and all prisoners move to its cadence. Everything revolves around the camp experience and the place, Auschwitz, is the main character.

Staging
Props are highlighted against a dark background, bringing an openness to the stage sets. This liberates the audience from the

artificial boundaries that scenery creates while enhancing a sense of timelessness. A high platform extends across the back third of the stage. The stage will be set with a minimum number of props, augmented by the actors bringing additional props onto the stage when they can seamlessly be incorporated into the scene. There are certain situations when the stage is set with multiple locations that work independently. The lighting moves from one highlighted area to another, sequencing the action as the scene unfolds. There is a basic duality to the structure of the play, yet all the elements are interwoven, and every situation is interconnected. The play is performed on two physical planes (platform and stage), in two time periods (present and past), and on two cognitive levels (Levi's awareness of the present and his perception of the past).

Transitions

The play is a one-act presentation. The transitions should take less than twenty seconds with a few exceptions. The scene changes will be made in a blackout environment (darkness) with the stagehands dressed in black, using night-vision goggles. Besides the setting-up and breaking-down of the scenes, the stagehands will also lead the actors on and off the stage. Maintaining a continuous pace and flow is essential to realize the story's progression, power, and purpose.

This is only a guide intended to move the reader beyond the dialogue by emphasizing the importance of visualizing the action and imagining the movement— seeing the terror through the eyes of the prisoners, perceiving their fear, and following their footsteps as their world is revealed and experienced. It is a world that transformed Primo Levi, leaving an indelible imprint on his soul that haunted and sustained him throughout his life.

PRIMO

CHARACTERS

Turin, 1987

Primo I - Primo Levi in his sixties
Lucia - Primo's wife
Attorney Giotto - Primo's attorney and friend
Mr. and Mrs. Mariano - Clients of Attorney Giotto
Gilberto - Journalist who interviews Primo
Waiter - Serves Primo and Gilberto in a restaurant
Voiceovers - Teacher and Alfonso, a student

Buna Camp Jewish Prisoners

Veteran Prisoners who understand how the camp works

Primo II - Primo as a young prisoner
Alberto - Primo's close friend
Shlomo - *Primo's Alter Ego*, demoted barracks clerk and labor squad worker, Lena's husband
Moshe - Has debilitating condition of swollen feet
The Greek - Worker on the trench digging squad
Nachman - Worker on the trench digging squad
Buna Kapo - Marches Buna prisoners to Birkenau
Tailor - Works with Feliks on the railroad track

New Jewish Prisoners who just arrived from Hungary

Miska - Teenager with a conspicuous gold crown tooth
Janko - Miska's father
Leib - Fragile young man wearing glasses
Joshua - Friend of Leib
Jozsef - Marches toward Birkenau
Henrik - Marches next to Jozsef toward Birkenau

Camp Scenes in Birkenau, 1944

German Personnel
    Captain Moll - Commandant's assistant
    Lieutenant Muller - Junior officer
    Corporal - In charge of the rear gate
    Sergeant - In charge of the Buna formation
    Otto - Guard of the Buna formation

Polish Prisoners who build the railroad track
    Borslaw - Kapo in charge
    Tomasz - Foreman
    Stanislaw - Worker
    Feliks - Worker

Jewish Prisoners at Birkenau
    Rubin - Kapo in charge of the gravel mound
    Izak - Foreman of the trench digging squad
    Abie - Prisoner/trader of warehouse merchandise
    Latrine Prisoner - Veteran prisoner in Birkenau
    Dentist - Prisoner who works in a ditch

Other Jewish Prisoners
    Lena - Shlomo's wife and a prisoner
    Abie's Father - Laborer from another camp who works on a large gravel cart
    Shlomo's Mother - Sings a Yiddish lullaby

Other Characters
    Barracks Leader - Conducts roll call at the Buna Camp
    SS Roll Call Officer - Buna Camp
    Sergi - Russian prisoner, foreman gravel mound
    Women (Dancers) - Transported to the gas

Incidental Characters
  Burning Pit Kapo
  Turntable Prisoner I
  Turntable Prisoner II
  Turntable Prisoner III
  Turntable Prisoner IV
  Prisoner I
  Prisoner II
  Prisoner III
  Hungarian Prisoner

Stage Directions
Downstage - The front of the stage nearest the audience.
Upstage - The back of the stage farthest from the audience.

Turin, Italy
1987

Scene I

Illuminated on a dark stage, Primo I and Lucia are standing near the permanent raised platform that extends across the back third of the stage. They are wearing nightshirts, with their legs bent and their heads tilted, leaning against their closed hands, asleep. Behind them, slowly coming into view at the back of the platform, is the shadowy image of the crematory chimney. The light fades on Lucia as Primo I becomes restless when a line of concrete fence posts connected by barbed wire is illuminated at the front of the platform. Wearing a prison uniform, Shlomo emerges out of the darkness. Standing next to Primo I he waits, but Primo I just sleeps.

SHLOMO
(Challenging)
Remember me?

Primo I becomes slightly more agitated but remains asleep. Shlomo frowns, and then snaps to attention removing his beret and slapping his hips; he shouts.

Prisoner 149785! Clerk, Barracks Fifteen— Buna Camp—
 (With hatred for the place)
Auschwitz.

He stares at Primo I, but again there is no reaction. Shaking his head, he moves away as Primo I fades into semi-darkness. He looks down to one side, searching the past and then stares at his raised hand.

In another life . . . another place . . . I was Shlomo.

Noticing the barbed wire, his body tightens.

But *here*!

Instantly, a formation of prisoners is illuminated on the other side of the stage. Shlomo puts on his beret, running to the formation.

STRAIGHTEN UP!

The prisoners straighten their ranks. Shlomo moves down the front of the formation counting the ranks. Suddenly, he stops. Plunging into the ranks, he pushes the prisoners aside until he reaches Alberto.

You Italian shit! Which one?

Alberto snaps to attention.

ALBERTO
Alberto, Clerk.

Shlomo motions toward the vacant space next to him.

SHLOMO
The other, Primo. Where is he?

Alberto shrugs; instantly Shlomo delivers a blow then begins leaving the ranks.

Fuck! It's the work squad if I don't find the bastard.

He moves down the front of the formation counting the ranks as the Barracks Leader approaches. Shlomo runs up to report.

The fucking Italian's missing.

The Barracks Leader smacks him across the face.

BARRACKS LEADER
Which one?

                                SHLOMO
Primo.

With an abrupt hand movement, the Barracks Leader demands to be taken to Alberto. Alberto raises his arm showing the tattooed number on his wrist. Taking out a small book, the Barracks Leader checks the number. An SS Officer walks toward the formation. Shlomo nudges the Barracks Leader and nods toward the Officer. They leave the ranks as Shlomo fades into the formation while the Barracks Leader stands in front of the prisoners, facing them.

                            BARRACKS LEADER
Caps off! At-ten-tion!

The prisoners remove their berets and slap their hips. The Barracks Leader does an about-face to the SS Officer as the light diminishes on the formation, leaving the Barracks Leader and SS Officer highlighted.

Barracks Fifteen!
  (Glancing down at the book)
Prisoner 1-7 4-5 1-7, absent!

The SS Officer slowly extends his open hand.

                              SS OFFICER
Really.

Taking the book, he silently reads the name and then looks up.

PRIMO LEVI!

                               PRIMO II
Present!

Instantly, Primo II is highlighted, standing near Primo I, dressed in black. The SS Officer returns the book as Primo II reluctantly walks to the formation.

Why! Why did I say that? Not here. No. No! Hate this place! How? How could I . . .

Smiling with a self-congratulatory nod, the SS Officer watches Primo II. Entering the ranks, Primo II stands in the empty space next to Alberto. Alberto welcomes him with a friendly nod while the SS Officer leaves.

What?

Alberto nervously looks around. Reaching into the hidden pocket inside his prison shirt, Alberto takes out a small piece of bread.

ALBERTO
Saved a piece of bread for you.

Alberto extends his hand.

PRIMO II
You don't understand! By staying, I survived!
    (To himself)
Can't be here.

Primo II stares at the bread for a few moments, and then takes it. He begins chewing. With a vacant expression, he mechanically flips the cloth cover on the black turtleneck he's wearing, exposing a yellow Jewish star. A whistle sounds. The Barracks Leader does an about-face.

BARRACKS LEADER
Caps on! Barracks Fifteen. Report to work squads! Dis-missed!

The prisoners move in different directions as the stage begins to slowly darken. Shlomo walks up to the Barracks Leader who points in the opposite direction. Shlomo stiffens, and then follows the other prisoners toward their work squads, going off stage. The Barracks Leader grabs another prisoner, Shlomo's replacement. They walk in the opposite direction of the work squads, exiting the stage. Primo I and Lucia reappear in their nightshirts, highlighted on the semi-darkened stage. Primo I is mumbling to himself as Lucia stares at him with growing concern. On the platform the prisoners are marching in place. Illuminated by a soft light, they move as shadows behind the barbed wire.

PRIMO I

How! How could this happen?

LUCIA

Are you all right?

PRIMO I

Oh— Just a dream.

LUCIA

You're so restless, tossing and turning.

PRIMO I

(Annoyed)
You know my dreams.

LUCIA

It's still early, try to sleep.

Lucia goes back to sleep as Primo I glances at the prisoners on the platform. Walking onto the stage, Primo II is holding a prison shirt in his hand. He is now wearing prison pants with the turtleneck and the beret on his shaved head. He passes Primo I, who watches him as he moves down stage. Primo II turns around staring at Primo I and notices the prisoners marching off the platform as it darkens. Seeing the formation entering the stage, Primo II puts on the prison shirt over the turtleneck with the black collar slightly showing. The prisoner formation crosses the stage in full light, collecting Primo II as it passes by. Primo I stares at the empty space where Primo II stood, and then watches the formation marching off stage.

Scene 2

Lucia, wearing an apron, stands in the kitchen preparing a breakfast tray. Sitting at the table, Primo I is reading the newspaper and sipping his coffee.

LUCIA

Lately, she only pecks at her food.

PRIMO I

It's just a phase my mother's going through.

LUCIA

The tray's ready! She'll complain if you're late.

Glancing at his watch, Primo I stands and walks toward the counter.

PRIMO I

My appointment with Giotto is at ten. I won't be able to spend much time with her.

LUCIA

Then she'll take to one of her moods, sulking for the rest of the day.

PRIMO I

I have a luncheon interview with the journalist from Rome.

He picks up the tray.

LUCIA

The one writing a book?

PRIMO I

Yes, it's our first meeting.

He begins walking out of the kitchen as Lucia watches him.

LUCIA
When it's over, come home and rest.

He stops near the edge of the kitchen.

PRIMO I
In the afternoon, I'm speaking to the history class at the high school. You know how I feel about those talks.

He leaves the kitchen as Lucia sighs.

Scene 3

A dancer, dressed as Primo I, stands on the top landing of a high staircase. Holding a small briefcase in his hand, he pantomimes closing his apartment door. He pauses, looking down the center of the stairwell to the bottom and then begins briskly walking down the stairs.

Scene 4

Attorney Giotto is sitting at his large desk across from Primo I, browsing a legal document. On one side of the office is the closed office door. On the other side at the back of the office is a bookcase filled with legal books. In front of the bookcase is a low table with a decorative plant placed in the middle. As Primo I and the Attorney talk, the other side of the office where the table and bookcase are, slowly darkens.

ATTORNEY GIOTTO
And most importantly, a title. I took the liberty to pencil in "Primo Levi Trust."

PRIMO I
I— don't want to use the trust to perpetuate my name.

ATTORNEY GIOTTO
It's a common practice.

PRIMO I
The books are my legacy.

ATTORNEY GIOTTO
Of course . . . I've always admired your insight in portraying the camps, especially your depiction of the prisoners you encountered.

PRIMO I
But they're gone. And the few of us left are fading. Time— time is our enemy now.

ATTORNEY GIOTTO
Time is everyone's enemy.

PRIMO I
This morning I thought of a name for the trust: "Alberto Fund."

ATTORNEY GIOTTO
Your comrade?

PRIMO I
Yes.

The Attorney corrects the document when his telephone rings.

ATTORNEY GIOTTO
Excuse me. Yes, Teresa? . . . He's not on the calendar. . . . All right, the other office.
  (To Primo)

Divorce, always a difficult situation! Perhaps, you can look over the stipulations while I see him for a moment. He seems a bit agitated.

PRIMO I

That's fine.

Handing Primo I the document, Attorney leaves. Primo I concentrates on the stipulations as two prisoners, Shlomo and Moshe appear, standing on each side of the low table, while the chimney is slowly highlighted.

SHLOMO

Nu! [*Yiddish: So!*]

Primo I looks up.

Big Shot. Mister Famous Writer. Does he think people care? About us?
   (Pulling his prison shirt)
About this!
   (Sadly looking upstage)
About the smoke from the chimney?

MOSHE

That dream, I had it again.

SHLOMO

Huh?

MOSHE

I return home dressed in real clothes but looking like this.
   (Staring at his emaciated hand)
And my friends ask . . . "Moshe, where have you been?" So I tell them about this place, and as I talk, one by one,
   (Surprised/hurt)
they turn away.

SHLOMO

Everyone has that dream. But Moshe, who's left at home?

Moshe nods despondently.

Nu! Mister Big-Shot. How can you explain this?
  (*Gesturing over his soiled uniform*)
A living cesspool, the walking odor of piss and shit— the stench of filth. There are no words that can explain this place— no language. DO YOU HEAR ME! . . .
  (*Sadly*)
No one will ever understand. . . .
  (*Turning to Moshe*)
I tell ya, Moshe, the only thing that keeps me going is Lena. If I could only remember which group she was in . . . when I left the ramp.

MOSHE

She's young. She must be in one of the camps.

SHLOMO

Every day, I ask.

MOSHE

Every day, there are more and more Hungarians. The camp is bursting at the seams!

SHLOMO

  (*Worried*)
Another selection.

Moshe, wearing camp clogs, lifts his swollen foot onto the low table, raising that pant leg.

MOSHE

With this, I won't make it. I'll be left in the barracks with the others while the rest of you go to your work squads.

SHLOMO

It doesn't look so bad.

MOSHE

Then a truck ride
 (Nods towards the chimney)
there.

SHLOMO

You worry too much. I've seen worse.
 (Touching Moshe's foot)
But leave me your bowl and spoon. I'll keep them for you.

Moshe agrees with a melancholy nod as a faint knock is heard. Instantly, Shlomo and Moshe disappear into darkness while the chimney remains illuminated. Attorney Giotto peeks in through the partially open door.

ATTORNEY GIOTTO

How are you doing, Primo?

PRIMO I

Huh, oh! . . . My mind must have wandered.

The Attorney walks in as Primo I stands, glancing at his watch.

It's late. I have a meeting at twelve.

ATTORNEY GIOTTO

Take the document with you. When you're ready, you'll make another appointment.

PRIMO I
Perhaps that's best. There's no reason to rush it.

He glances at the chimney.

Scene 5

The reception office as the Marianos, a middle-aged couple, walk in. They nod to the receptionist and sit on the couch. Attorney Giotto and Primo I enter. Noticing the Marianos, the Attorney hesitates for a moment, and then addresses them with a warm smile.

ATTORNEY GIOTTO
I'll be with you in a moment.

The Marianos acknowledge the Attorney.

Teresa, will you put Mr. Levi's papers in an envelope.

MR. MARIANO
Maybe we should wait. Postpone making the will.

MRS. MARIANO
Now, Vito. We agreed.

Mr. Mariano nods, awkwardly shifting his position on the couch. The receptionist hands Primo I the envelope and he slips it into his briefcase. Attorney Giotto shakes Primo I's hand.

ATTORNEY GIOTTO
Good-bye, Primo.

MRS. MARIANO
That's Primo Levi, the writer.

MR. MARIANO
What did he write?

MRS. MARIANO
I don't remember. He was on television accepting the Campiello Prize.

MR. MARIANO
What does he write about?

Primo I walks past the Marianos.

MRS. MARIANO
The death camps.

Mr. Mariano frowns as he stares at Primo I, walking off stage.

In the transition just before the next scene opens.

MRS. MARIANO
(Off stage)
What do you expect . . .

Scene 6

The dancer playing Primo I slowly walks onto the empty stage opposite the chimney as black smoke billows from the stack. Primo II enters the stage opposite Primo I.

                    MRS. MARIANO
(Off stage)
He's a Jew.

They stare at each other for a moment. Then Primo I turns toward the chimney. Two prisoners join Primo II as they begin marching in place. Alberto is on one side and Joshua on the other. Primo II turns to Alberto.

                    PRIMO II
Where do you think we're going?

                    ALBERTO
(Worried)
Smell it?

Primo II takes a deep breath.

                    PRIMO II
They wouldn't march us there. They'd use trucks. Better control that way.

                    ALBERTO
We're still strong enough to work.

                    PRIMO II
Too many new prisoners in the group.
    (Turning to Joshua)
Hungarian?

                    JOSHUA
From Sárvár. And you?

                    PRIMO II
We're Italian. Primo.
    (Indicating with a nod)
Alberto.

JOSHUA

(Rather loudly)
Italian!

ALBERTO

(Hushed but firm)
Quiet, you fool!

PRIMO II

Speak softly but always keep your eyes open!

Leib, wearing glasses, walks up behind Primo II, marching in place. The Greek and another prisoner move up on either side of Leib. Leib leans forward.

LEIB

What's that smell, Josh?

JOSHUA

Can't tell.

GREEK

(Loudly)
It's called "the bakery."

Inquisitively, Primo I turns staring at the prisoners.

LEIB

Strange smell. What do they bake?

The Greek chuckles. Another three prisoners move in behind Leib's row. Shlomo is behind Leib with Moshe next to him. The formation begins moving across the stage as more prisoners join the ranks. Suddenly, Shlomo hits Leib in the back.

SHLOMO
Keep in step! You Hungarian shit!

Leib switches step, followed by Shlomo and then the other prisoners in their row.

MOSHE
Easy, Shlomo! They only came yesterday.

In the next row Jozsef looks around making a funny face. He turns to Henrik, the prisoner next to him.

JOZSEF
Smell something?

HENRIK
I heard "the bakery."

JOZSEF
Bakery?

Jozsef takes a deep breath, shaking his head.

Smells like a tannery. I know, we had one in our town.

MOSHE
Forget your town! Forget everything! Here—

SHLOMO
Here, everything's the same— *shit*!

JOZSEF
What did they say?

HENRIK
They said, we're shit!

JOZSEF

Hmm.

The column passes Primo I going off stage and onto the dimly lit platform, marching toward the chimney. Primo I walks in sync with the prisoners. Affected by the rising smoke, he moves across the stage with the same apprehension as the prisoners. Miska, a teenager in the ranks, turns to his father, Janko.

MISKA

Father, what did they say that smell is?

JANKO

It's nothing, Miska. Nothing that concerns us.

Slowly the back of the stage turns a rose color as the prisoners move like shadows against this backdrop. SS Captain Moll appears on stage with the chimney behind him. He taps his leg with a riding crop to the prisoners' cadence, and then smiles as he watches Primo I walk by.

LEIB

What are they burning?

MOSHE

We . . . are burning.

The stage darkens, except for Captain Moll, as the sound of a wrench striking a metal rail is heard. Tomasz is illuminated, sitting off to the side of the stage, idly swinging a large wrench against a railroad rail. Noticing the Captain, he begins swinging the wrench in earnest. Captain Moll approaches. Tomasz drops the wrench and jumps up, removing his beret and slapping his hips.

TOMASZ

(Shouts)
Prisoner 157658.

CAPTAIN MOLL
What are you doing, making all that racket?

TOMASZ
Preparing the turntable for the cremo cars, sir.

CAPTAIN MOLL
Will it be ready for today's production?

TOMASZ
(Enthusiastic)
Jawohl, sir!

CAPTAIN MOLL
Where's Lieutenant Muller?

TOMASZ
At the burning pits, sir.

Captain Moll leaves.

Scene 7

SS Lieutenant Muller is standing on the platform looking upstage at a pit while the prisoners are unloading a wagon full of wood.

LIEUTENANT MULLER
Kapo! Stack the wood close to the edge. Five piles per pit. One for each layer. Leave room for the wagons!
(Noticing Captain Moll approaching)
The pace, Kapo!

BURNING PIT KAPO
You filthy swine, MOVE!

The Kapo makes threatening gestures as he pushes a few prisoners. Captain Moll walks up as the Lieutenant salutes him.

LIEUTENANT MULLER
Sir, the pits are ready.

The Captain returns the salute and then stares at the pits for a moment.

CAPTAIN MOLL
I want an additional wood pile at each end of every pit. More fuel is always required when the items have too little flesh-on-the-bone.

He turns around facing downstage; the Lieutenant follows.

The first transports from Budapest are arriving today. This is only the beginning. . . . You heard, the front's moving.

They stare at each other, then the Lieutenant nods with a concerned expression.

The materials have arrived. Time's pressing! It's imperative the new track be up and running. You'll have extra prisoners from the Buna Camp. Make sure the kapos integrate them with their work crews.

LIEUTENANT MULLER
Yes, sir.

The Captain looks up at the sky.

CAPTAIN MOLL
I want the pipe trench near the main road dug out. That drainage problem has to be corrected.

CORPORAL
(Off stage)
Open the gate!

CAPTAIN MOLL
Buna prisoners.

In the transition just before the next scene opens.

BUNA KAPO
(Shouts from off stage)
Straighten up! Left! Left! Left, right, left!

Scene 8

The Corporal stands by the back gate of the Birkenau Camp as the Buna Kapo marches by with the formation of prisoners. Near the Corporal is an empty wooden ammo box covered with black markings of its past contents and rope handles at each end. The Buna Sergeant walks up to the Corporal.

CORPORAL
Are you from Buna?

SERGEANT
Yes, long march. My feet are killing me!

CORPORAL
Now you can rest. The Captain wants them formed up over there and your guard on the perimeter fence.
(Looking away)
He's coming!

                    SERGEANT
(Shouts)
Kapo! Form them up there!

                    BUNA KAPO
(Shouts)
Left turn, march!

                    SERGEANT
Who's the Captain?

                    CORPORAL
Moll . . . A specialist on burning pits. The crematories can't keep up with all the transports.

                    SERGEANT
Hungarians?

                    BUNA KAPO
(Shouts)
Halt! Right face!

                    CORPORAL
Yeah, we're busier now than ever!

The Sergeant takes a deep breath.

                    SERGEANT
Does it always smell like this?

                    CORPORAL
What smell?

The Sergeant gives him a look of disbelief.

BUNA KAPO

(Shouts)
Straighten the ranks.

SERGEANT

Hafta go.

The Sergeant walks to the formation and stands in front of the Kapo.

BUNA KAPO

All present!
(Softly)
He's here.

The Kapo moves into the ranks as Captain Moll walks up.

SERGEANT

Caps off! At-ten-tion!

The prisoners remove their berets and slap their hips. The Sergeant does an about-face to the Captain, saluting him.

Sir! Buna Camp work squad.

The Captain returns the salute. The Corporal grabs two prisoners from the ranks. He points to the wooden box. The prisoners carry it to the front of the ranks. The Captain points with his riding crop and the prisoners set the box down. They return to the formation as the Captain steps on the box. In silence, the Captain slowly stares at the formation, viewing it from right to left as he taps his leg with the riding crop. He then looks straight ahead.

CAPTAIN MOLL

You were brought here for an important job. Today you will finish laying the railway track from the crematory turntable to the river. This job will be completed successfully in the time prescribed.

Each prisoner must give everything he has, otherwise it will go badly for you. DO YOU UNDERSTAND?

PRISONERS

JAWOHL!

Scene 9

Kapo Borslaw stands on the empty stage and watches Kapo Rubin approaching. Rubin ignores Borslaw as they wait, silently displaying their animosity toward each other. Lieutenant Muller walks up.

LIEUTENANT MULLER

The materials have arrived. The Commandant wants the track completed by the end of the day.

Rubin clicks his heels.

RUBIN

Then it will be done!

Borslaw sneers at Rubin.

BORSLAW

We'll be using the track by the end of the day.

LIEUTENANT MULLER

We have extra prisoners from the Buna Camp. Integrate them with your crews. Kapo Borslaw, make sure Tomasz supervises the laying of the track. I don't want any surprises when the cars roll down the hill.

BORSLAW

I'll make sure it will be done correctly.

                    LIEUTENANT MULLER
Kapo Rubin, have a squad of prisoners work on the pipe trench near the main road.

                    RUBIN
We'll begin immediately!

                    LIEUTENANT MULLER
Regulations require the Buna prisoners back at their camp by sunset. It's a long march, so they will be leaving early. Be aware of that when setting the pace!

Scene 10

Tomasz, Stanislaw, and Feliks are standing outside a small wooden building with the sign TOOLS. On the opposite side of the stage, a group of prisoners are idly standing around as black smoke rises from the chimney. Kapo Borslaw enters near the group of prisoners. He hesitates, staring at the prisoners, and then continues toward the toolshed. Noticing the Kapo, Tomasz, Stanislaw, and Feliks quickly start organizing the tools lying around the building.

                    BORSLAW
   (Shouts)
Tomasz!

Tomasz runs up. Borslaw nods toward the prisoners.

Start organizing those prisoners into rail laying crews. The tracks have to be put down and working by this evening.

                    TOMASZ
What's the hurry, Kapo?

(Nods towards the chimney)
The Jews aren't going anywhere.

                        BORSLAW
(Slowly with anger)
Don't— bust— my— balls over this!

Tomasz quickly shows his regret. Borslaw looks back at the prisoners standing around, then turns to Tomasz speaking in a friendlier tone.

You know, Tomasz, I like you. You're a smart kid. But that's not why I made you foreman.

                        TOMASZ
Why, then?

                        BORSLAW
I like the way you tell stories. When this is over . . .
  (Turning towards the chimney)
if you survive, you'll be able to tell what happened here.

                        TOMASZ
I intend to.

                        BORSLAW
Good. Then make sure you're not joining the Jews for a ride down to the river.

                        TOMASZ
The track will be ready today, Kapo!

Borslaw nods and leaves.

  (Shouts)
Feliks!

Feliks runs up. Tomasz nods toward the prisoners.

Organize those prisoners into a work squad. You're in charge of putting the ties down.

FELIKS

(Enthusiastically)
Yes, railway foreman!

Scene ii

The Sergeant is rubbing his sore feet as he sits on a bench off to the side of the stage. His knapsack and old boots are at the end of the bench while his rifle leans upright against it. On the other side of the stage is a pile of railroad ties. On the platform, prisoners are moving wheelbarrows, pantomiming delivering gravel for the track bed. While other prisoners pantomime leveling the gravel with their shovels, Tomasz supervises the work. Feliks marches a formation past the Sergeant.

FELIKS

Pick up the pace!

The formation approaches the railroad ties.

Right turn! . . . Halt! . . . Right face!

Walking arrogantly in front of the ranks.

Listen up! Two prisoners per tie. Carry them to the rail bed. Place them . . . forty centimeters apart. You'll start at the turntable.

Pointing toward the unseen turntable.

Jews! Look where I'm pointing!

The prisoners look toward the turntable as the Sergeant notices Feliks's new shoes. He glumly stares at his old boots.

You'll move on the double.

The prisoners groan.

We must finish before lunch!

SERGEANT
(Shouts)
You!

Feliks turns toward the Sergeant.

Are you deaf?

Feliks runs up to the Sergeant, removing his beret and slapping his hips.

FELIKS
Yes, Corporal.

The Sergeant points to the chevrons on his sleeve.

SERGEANT
Sergeant!

FELIKS
Yes, Sergeant!

On the platform, Tomasz notices Feliks talking to the Sergeant.

SERGEANT

Oh, at ease. I was noticing your shoes. They're very nice. Where did you get such fine shoes?

Tomasz studies the prisoners working on the rail bed.

FELIKS

In camp.

SERGEANT

So, you get shoes like that!

FELIKS

Things are better now. The more transports, the more choices.

SERGEANT

Ah!
(Picks up his boots)
Look! Look what I have to wear.

Feliks stares at the boots. Tomasz grabs one of the prisoners, Alberto. He points to Feliks and the Sergeant as he speaks to Alberto.

FELIKS

They— they are old.

Indulging in self-pity, the Sergeant stares at the boots. Alberto runs off the platform. Shaking his head, the Sergeant sets the boots down next to the bench.

SERGEANT

It would be nice to have a good pair of shoes. In the Buna Camp, all the prisoners wear those shitty clogs. When they arrive, they always leave their good shoes here, at Birkenau! But I never thought they were that nice.

FELIKS
Yes, they are good. I was told they are handmade in the best Hungarian style.

Lifting his foot, slowly rotating it slightly to each side.

Nice design, eh?

On the sly, the Sergeant lifts his foot measuring it to the shoe and smiles, then lowers his foot. He nods to Feliks, acknowledging the shoes' good design. Then he looks down at his old boots, quietly staring for a few moments, before looking up.

SERGEANT
Sell me your shoes! You can always get more.

Surprised, Feliks becomes fidgety.

FELIKS
Um . . . um . . . Why? Why, I can't do that.
 (Starting to regain his composure)
They're camp property!

Annoyed, the Sergeant frowns; then slowly, his expression softens.

SERGEANT
It's all right, as long as no one knows. I have some extra bread.

The Sergeant reaches over, sliding his knapsack across the bench to his side.

FELIKS
I'm not hungry.

SERGEANT
Maybe a small piece of meat?

He looks through his knapsack as Alberto runs up, removing his beret and slapping his hips.

ALBERTO
(Shouts)
Rail layer! You and your squad are wanted by the tracks, immediately!

SERGEANT
Huh?

The Sergeant looks up at Alberto as Feliks turns, leaving on the double.

Wait. Wait! But the shoes?

Moving his rifle closer, the Sergeant glares at Alberto. Feliks hurriedly gathers the prisoners into a formation as Tomasz watches from the rail bed. Alberto turns to leave.

(Hissing)
Where are you going?

ALBERTO
I was told to deliver the message and report back at once, Sergeant!

The Sergeant looks toward Feliks's squad as they quickly begin marching off stage leaving the railroad ties behind. He then scrutinizes Alberto, moving down his uniform, and stares at his muddy clogs, shaking his head.

SERGEANT
Get outta here!

Alberto leaves on the double.

Scene 12

Kapo Rubin approaches the shallow trench as ten prisoners wait next to it. They are lined up by height, holding shovels. Primo II, Leib, Joshua, Shlomo, the Greek, and Nachman are in this group.

RUBIN
Good! This is a very important job.

Rubin walks to the middle of the trench, surveys it, and then turns toward the prisoners.

You.
  (Pointing to the tallest, Leib)
The trench.

Staring straight ahead, Leib is unaware he has been picked. The foreman, Izak, a teenager, elbows Leib in the stomach with a slight blow and points toward the trench. Leib moves into the trench, standing at one end.

The pipe will slope down to the road. Let's say, two meters deep, there.

Rubin points to one end of the trench while looking at Izak. Izak acknowledges with a nod. Rubin walks along the trench until he stands above Leib.

And— one meter above his head. He's the measuring stick.

Scene 13

Tomasz and Stanislaw are standing by the toolshed. Abie appears near the crematory chimney as black smoke rises from the stack.

> TOMASZ

You'll have to take care of the ties. He can't go back there!

> STANISLAW

The fool's worthless. He'll get us all killed!

Feliks walks up.

> FELIKS

I'm here!

Tomasz nods to Feliks, then notices Abie approaching.

> TOMASZ

Your friend's coming.

Feliks moves around the side of the shed as Stanislaw grabs his sleeve.

> STANISLAW

A deal's a deal. Pay him and get rid of him.

Abie walks up, nods to Tomasz, and then looks at Feliks's new shoes.

> ABIE

How's the fit?

> FELIKS

They nearly got me killed!

> ABIE

Same thing happened to their previous owner.

> STANISLAW

Pay him! Damn it!

Feliks takes a handful of cigarettes out of the hidden pocket inside his shirt. He turns his back to Abie, counting out five and putting the rest back. He hands them to Abie. Abie looks at the cigarettes in his hand and smiles. He then looks up at Feliks, nodding menacingly toward his outstretched hand. Stanislaw angrily gives Feliks a hard nudge.

Finish it!

Feliks fumbles in his pocket, and then hands Abie two more cigarettes. Abie turns to Tomasz while putting the cigarettes into the hidden pocket inside his shirt. Abie nods toward the unseen guard on the fence line.

ABIE
Careful of that Buna guard . . . has a light trigger finger. He's called Crazy Otto. Word has it, he has a knack for getting three-day passes.

TOMASZ
How?

ABIE
(Mockingly)
A reward for killing a prisoner trying to escape.

TOMASZ
We'll be careful.

Abie leaves as Tomasz stares at the unseen guard.

Scene 14

Feliks sits on a bench inside the tool shed holding one of his shoes. Sadly, he stares at the shiny shoe for a few moments. He then puts his hand into the bowl next to him and begins covering the shoe with mud.

Scene 15

The Corporal is staring out the open window of the guardhouse watching Abie approach as black smoke rises from the chimney. As Abie walks past, the Corporal reaches through the window, grabbing his arm.

CORPORAL

Where's the shirt you promised me?

ABIE

I had the most beautiful shirt. Silk!

Abie raises his arms measuring the Corporal's upper torso. As Abie does this, he stares at the Corporal's hand grasping him. The Corporal releases his grip. Imitating a tailor with a measuring tape, Abie lifts the Corporal's arm.

It was a perfect fit. Just as I was going to organize it, Captain Moll appeared!

The Corporal becomes alarmed.

Don't worry. There'll be more transports tomorrow. I'll get you one of those handmade, Parisian shirts, by way of Hungary. After all, we Jews always wear our best to the gas. Don't forget, a half-liter of vodka.

CORPORAL

Don't you forget! I'm going on furlough soon.

ABIE

I'll take care of you.

Kapo Rubin approaches. He motions to Abie to join him nearby, out of the Corporal's line of sight.

RUBIN
I want to remove a gold crown.

ABIE
A little something for the future, Kapo?

Rubin nods towards the chimney.

RUBIN
That's our future.

Rubin stares long and hard at Abie. Abie glances at the chimney.

ABIE
Who has it?

Rubin points toward the unseen gravel mound.

RUBIN
That kid at the gravel mound.

ABIE
The one standing next to the old man?

RUBIN
The old man's his father.

ABIE
Are they from the Buna Camp?

RUBIN
(Reluctantly)
Yeah.

ABIE
You know what that means?

Rubin frowns.

The only way to get it is if the kid cooperates.

RUBIN
You'll talk to 'im.

He stares hard at Abie.

ABIE
(Slowly)
Okay.

RUBIN
I want you to get a specialist from the cremo.

Abie shakes his head.

ABIE
Too risky! Transports are arriving all the time. The SS are everywhere.

Rubin looks around, then points.

RUBIN
See the prisoners in that ditch?

Abie glances at the unseen ditch.

ABIE
So?

RUBIN
One of 'em is a dentist.

Abie stares at the unseen ditch.

ABIE
I can tell by the way he swings his pick.

RUBIN
You'll get five rations of bread.

Abie thinks for a moment.

ABIE
How about the kid?

RUBIN
Offer 'im two. I'll take care of it.

ABIE
Send him to the latrine.

RUBIN
I'll arrange it. Oh. Get a good pair of shoes for my foreman, Izak.

ABIE
It's dif-fi—

RUBIN
Like you got for that stupid Pole! The one who works on the rail crew.
   (Looking down at Abie's shoes)
Same size as those.

Rubin stares until Abie nods reluctantly; Rubin leaves.

Scene 16

Standing on the gravel mound, Sergi supervises the work as Kapo Rubin approaches. Before reaching the gravel mound, Rubin stops and observes the prisoners waiting in line with their empty wheelbarrows. On the other side of the stage is a wooden building with the sign LATRINE.

RUBIN

(Shouts)
Hey! You!

Each prisoner stares at the Kapo in fear. Sergi looks up, smiling.

SERGI

Which one, Kapo?

Sergi moves his arm along the line of prisoners, pointing at each one for a moment. The prisoners now stare at Sergi waiting anxiously for his arm to move past them. He's pointing at Moshe.

RUBIN

That sack of shit!

SERGI

Go!

Moshe leaves his wheelbarrow, slowly running up to the Kapo.

RUBIN

You know where the latrine is?

MOSHE

Yes, Kapo! . . . Where?

Rubin grabs Moshe's arm, swings him around, pointing to the latrine.

                        RUBIN

I'm appointing you "latrine chaperone." Any attempted escapes, any unnecessary lingering, and you'll return to Buna on a stretcher.

He swings him around again.

See that kid over there?

Moshe looks toward the prisoners, confused.

                        MOSHE

Which one, Kapo?

                        RUBIN

The kid next to the old man. You see 'im?

                        MOSHE

(Concentrating harder)
Yes, Kapo.

                        RUBIN

I want you to escort 'im to the latrine.

Moshe cautious, hesitates.

Still here!

Moshe runs over to Miska, tapping him on the shoulder.

                        MOSHE

Come with me!

Miska, perplexed, looks at Moshe and then to his father, Janko. Janko notices the Kapo staring at Miska and nods "go on."

Forget your wheelbarrow. Let's go!

They walk away as Rubin leaves and the gravel mound fades into darkness.

MISKA
Where are we going?

Moshe ignores him.

Scene 17

Nachman stands with his shovel by the edge of the trench looking down at the prisoners digging. He stares at Leib for a few moments. Leib, whose head is now below the rim, continues digging at a faster pace than the others.

NACHMAN
You! You in the front of the trench, "the Marker."

Leib looks up.

Stop.
   (Addressing the other prisoners)
He's too deep. You have to start passing the dirt back, then throw it out.
   (Motioning to Joshua and Primo II)
You two pass.
   (Pointing to Shlomo)
He'll throw it out.

SHLOMO

All right.
(Turning toward Leib)
Make sure you slow the pace.
(To himself)
Stupid shits.

PRIMO II

Listen, Marker.

LEIB

Leib.

PRIMO II

Listen, Leib. Now, we all work together and you alone set the rhythm. So . . . slow the pace.

JOSHUA

They're right, Leib.

Leib nods in agreement.

Scene 18

In the dimly lit interior of the latrine, a prisoner sits on the end commode of five commode openings on a long, narrow, box-like concrete bench. Giving the impression of a sunbather, his face is raised up and his eyes are closed. Moshe and Miska enter the latrine and wait for their eyes to adjust as the interior light slowly brightens. Abie is quietly standing in the shadows, near Moshe.

MOSHE

Sit next to him.

MISKA

Why?

MOSHE

Who knows?

Miska accidentally nudges the prisoner as he sits down next to him. The prisoner opens one eye and then the other. He lifts Miska's left arm with his right hand, staring at his number.

LATRINE PRISONER

Phew! Such a high-number!
  (Turning slowly, looking straight ahead)
Yesterday, praying over the Talmud and now, sitting over a pile of shit— in Birkenau!
  (Bursts out laughing, then stops abruptly. Turning slowly to his right, looking past Miska, as if searching)
Where is God?
  (Slowly looking straight ahead)
Where is God?
  (Slowly to his left)
Where is God?

Miska pulls his arm away, provoking the Latrine Prisoner.

You Hungarians. You stupid shits! Didn't you hear of this place? In 1944!
  (Looking straight ahead)
Ah! You are lucky to have come so late.
  (Begins rocking in a self-absorbed state)
Oy [Oy-eeee] . . . When I came, there was nothing
  (Stops rocking, turns to Miska)
not even blankets in minus twenty-degree weather. Every morning, the bodies were collected by the hundreds. And in the daytime the kapos had orders— yes, orders!—
  (Slowly looking straight ahead)

To kill a certain number of us.
   (Begins rocking in a self-absorbed state)
Oy [Oy-eeee] . . . How we disappeared.
   (Stops rocking, turns to Miska)
Like smoke, going up a chimney.
   (Inwardly asking himself)
Where is God? Where is God?
   (Moving his face closer to Miska)
And the selections!
   (Intonating into a descending pitch)
Mer-ci-less!
   (Instantly bursts out laughing, stops abruptly)
Have you been through a selection, boy?

                              MISKA
Stop it!

                        LATRINE PRISONER
Oy, you are lucky.

                              MISKA
Please, stop it!

                        LATRINE PRISONER
Don't worry. You won't make it. You'll go up the chimney . . . ash and smoke.
   (With sadness looking straight ahead)
Like all the others.

Miska looks to Moshe.

                              MOSHE
Enough, low number.

Out of the shadows, Abie's hand gently grabs Moshe's shoulder. Moshe stares at him. Abie walks over to the commodes as Miska stealthily starts to slide away. Abie sits down next to Miska, wedging him between himself and the Latrine Prisoner who now rocks back and forth, staring straight ahead.

LATRINE PRISONER
Where is God? Where is God?

ABIE
I want your gold crown, kid.

Miska stares at Abie.

LATRINE PRISONER
(Sympathetic to Miska's plight)
Where is God?

He stops rocking.

ABIE
You'll get two rations of bread for it.

MISKA
Can't.

ABIE
Make it easy on yourself.

MISKA
Can't eat without it.

ABIE
What do you get to eat here, huh?

LATRINE PRISONER
(Looking straight ahead)
Today. This place is a paradise.

MISKA
I . . . I have to ask my father.

ABIE
I want an answer right after lunch.

LATRINE PRISONER
Not like the old days when I came.

ABIE
Make it the right answer, or it will go badly for you.

LATRINE PRISONER
Where is God?
(Challenging)
Where are you!?
(Leans forward, right arm bent, hand clenched into a fist, looking up)
WHERE ARE YOU!?

Scene 19

The prisoners on the platform are each holding an empty bowl, waiting in front of the large soup cauldron for the servers to begin as smoke rises from the chimney. Down stage center, Primo I and Gilberto, the journalist, are sitting at a restaurant table covered with a white cloth, eating. On one side of the stage is the outside wall of the toolshed where the three rail layers are settling in with their food. The soup line begins moving as prisoners' bowls are filled and they are given a portion of bread. They continue onto the sloping hillside that extends from the platform to the stage, with the chimney behind it. They are sitting down in ranks of five, with each prisoner leaning back against the upright bent legs of the prisoner behind him. The light fades on the restaurant table and hillside.

TOMASZ
With most of the ties down, I think we can make it.

STANISLAW
Still seems touch and go.

TOMASZ
You finish setting up the tracks. We'll connect them.
 (Looking at Feliks)
You take one side, I'll take the other. Don't fuck up!

Sadly, Feliks stares at his mud-caked shoes.

FELIKS
They're ruined. I've never had such fine shoes. Never!

STANISLAW
But you're alive!

TOMASZ
And stay away from that Sergeant! Stanis, have you heard any more about the uprising?

STANISLAW
Warsaw's bleeding! The Germans are destroying the city.

TOMASZ
The Russians?

STANISLAW
Still outside . . . *waiting*. But you already know that.

TOMASZ
They'll go in. They will! . . . Poor Warsaw.

STANISLAW
Amen.

The light fades on the toolshed. In a dim light, Primo I and Gilberto are still eating as the sloping hillside becomes highlighted. The prisoners are drinking their soup and eating their bread. The veterans are holding their bowls under their chins, so that when biting into their bread the crumbs fall into the soup. Alberto, sitting in front of Primo II, pauses after a spoonful of soup.

ALBERTO
Where are you working?

PRIMO II
In a ditch on the other side of the fence. You?

ALBERTO
On the rail bed.

PRIMO II
Crazy Otto guarding us.

ALBERTO
The Buna guard!

PRIMO II
Yes.

ALBERTO
Maybe I can help. The foreman owes me a favor, but you never know.

PRIMO II

Try.

The light fades from the hillside as the restaurant table is highlighted. A busboy walks to the table with a tray and stand. He clears the dishes away, leaving with the filled tray and taking the stand with him as the waiter approaches. The waiter starts scraping the surface of the tablecloth, ushering bread crumbs onto a small tray. Primo I studies the movement of the crumbs across the table. Gilberto observes Primo I's intense concentration on this simple restaurant routine. The waiter finishes and then looks up.

WAITER

Gentlemen, some dessert?

PRIMO I

They make the finest tiramisu in Turin.

Gilberto pats his stomach.

GILBERTO

Perhaps we can split a piece?

PRIMO I

I always end my meal with bread.

Gilberto is surprised.

GILBERTO

I'll have the tiramisu.

WAITER

An espresso, Mr. Levi?

PRIMO I

Please.

WAITER

Sir?

GILBERTO

Coffee.
(Pointing to the water glass)
Water.

The waiter searches the dining room for the water boy.

WAITER

(Slightly angry)
Pedro, over here!

The light dims on the table as the hillside is illuminated with Miska sitting in front of his father, who is beginning to doze.

MISKA

Father.

JANKO

Huh.

MISKA

They— they want my gold crown.

JANKO

Who?

MISKA

I don't know. We went to the latrine and this other prisoner said he wanted my gold crown. He gives two rations of bread.

JANKO

Some of these prisoners are worse than the guards!

MISKA
I told him, I have to ask you.

JANKO
I don't think it's a wise thing to do. After all, how could he take your crown? Where would he do it? I haven't seen any dental offices here. Hmm . . . And I've heard those who go to the infirmary seldom return. It doesn't sound good. You'll tell him no.

MISKA
He said it would go badly for me if I refused.

JANKO
How can it be worse than it is now?
  (Bending down awkwardly to see Miska's face)
How? . . . You did the right thing, Miska, by asking me. You'll tell him no.
  (Leaning back)
Now, don't worry about it. It's settled. Let's try to get some sleep. Lunchtime seems so short, and work so long.

They close their eyes and instantly doze off. The light fades on the hillside as the waiter brings the dessert and coffee to the table. He places the tiramisu in front of Gilberto and his coffee off to the side. He then serves Primo I his espresso. The light fades from the table and the toolshed is highlighted with the three rail layers. Having finished eating, Stanislaw's eyes begin to close as his head nods while Feliks looks up at the sky.

FELIKS
Think we'll see the sun?

STANISLAW
Huh.
  (Looking up at the sky)
Don't know. It's touch and go.

TOMASZ
Rain or shine, we'll be working our asses off! Those cremo cars have to be running down to the river by day's end.

Stanislaw turns toward the chimney.

STANISLAW
You're educated, Tomasz. Think the bastards will pay for what they're doing?

He nods toward the chimney. Tomasz looks at Stanislaw for a moment and then glances at the chimney.

TOMASZ
When this is over?

STANISLAW
Yeah.

TOMASZ
I think those who are caught will pay, according to the laws of man's justice. But for us? It will never be enough.

STANISLAW
They should suffer the way we suffer!

TOMASZ
  (To himself)
Never enough.
  (Turning toward the chimney)
Never enough.

Feliks takes out a small apple. Tomasz stares as Feliks gets ready to cut it.

(Forcefully as an order)
Quarter it!

FELIKS

But there are only three of us!

TOMASZ

One slice for the Jew, who saved your ass.

FELIKS

Well, I don't—

STANISLAW

Cut it four ways!

Feliks begrudgingly slices the apple. Tomasz watches as Feliks puts the extra apple slice into the hidden pocket inside his shirt. Then Tomasz looks up at the sky.

TOMASZ

I'd settle for just a little sunshine.

STANISLAW

Would be nice.

Their eyes start to close as Feliks quietly scrapes the mud from his shoes. The light fades from the toolshed as the restaurant table is highlighted. Gilberto takes his last bite of the cake.

GILBERTO

Excellent tiramisu.

Gilberto becomes a little uneasy as he gently wipes his mouth with his napkin.

This isn't part of the interview.

                    PRIMO I

But it is another question.

                    GILBERTO

(Hesitantly)
I was wondering. How do you deal with . . . the recurrence of genocide?

                    PRIMO I

I've come to the conclusion . . . it is part of the human fabric.

                    GILBERTO

You mean it has always been with us?

                    PRIMO I

Always? . . . I don't know. But now it always seems to be hovering in the background, waiting.

                    GILBERTO

For the right moment?

                    PRIMO I

Or the right conditions.
(Long pause)
Let me share a thought with you. It came to me one evening when I was in my study after a trying day at work. Another genocide had occurred. The newspaper contained several articles with the usual descriptions. After reading the details, I thumbed through the pages and happened on a minor story. It was about the recent discovery of a Neanderthal settlement that was only thirty thousand years old, which meant they lived in the same milieu as our ancestors.

GILBERTO

Coexisting.

PRIMO I

Yes. Then our ancestors took a leap in their development, intellectually . . . and the competition disappeared.

GILBERTO

You mean annihilated?

PRIMO I

I wondered, did we cross an irrevocable line? . . . That night, in the solitude of my study, I seemed to feel their presence, as if they came with us through time. That . . . their last desperate scream was forever etched on our souls.

GILBERTO

Like a curse?

Primo I nods ambiguously.

PRIMO I

It's a strange thought.

GILBERTO

It is my belief that we're capable of breaking that cycle.

A slight smile comes over Primo I's face. He turns away from Gilberto, looking upstage.

PRIMO I

I wonder.

He looks down at the small piece of bread on the bread plate. Picking it up, he turns it around, observing it as if it were a gem.

Sometimes, Alberto and I would play a game. Discussing the value of saving our last bite.

> GILBERTO
> I imagine, it was a way of exhibiting your will to resist.

Primo I and Gilberto fade into darkness as the hillside is highlighted. Primo II and Alberto are each holding up their last piece of bread.

> ALBERTO
> Ah! The end.

> PRIMO II
> So tiny.

Simultaneously, they chew their last morsel, relishing its flavor. Alberto looks up.

> ALBERTO
> Maybe today the sun will win.

He adjusts his position to catch the thin rays of the sun.

> PRIMO II
> Maybe.

Primo II leans back getting a better angle on the sun's rays. They close their eyes and instantly doze off. All the prisoners are asleep except for Shlomo. Shlomo fights the hunger gnawing at his withered body as he stares at his last bite of bread and then slips it into the hidden pocket inside his shirt. The light fades from the hillside, the restaurant table with Primo I and Gilberto disappears under the platform. Kapo Borslaw turns the corner of the toolshed, which is now highlighted, finding the three rail layers asleep. He gently nudges the foreman's shoe with his foot. Tomasz looks up.

BORSLAW
Will you be finished by the end of the day?

TOMASZ
Yes, Kapo.

BORSLAW
They didn't give us potato and turnip soup for nothing. If those cars aren't rolling down the track, it will go badly for all of us.

TOMASZ
We will finish, Kapo!

A whistle sounds. Lunch is over and the prisoners reluctantly drag themselves up. In the mass of moving prisoners, Shlomo seeks out Moshe.

SHLOMO
Moshe, you're the latrine chaperone?

Moshe nods and Shlomo slips the bread into his hand.

Take me to the latrine on one of your trips.

MOSHE
Where are you?

SHLOMO
In a ditch just beyond the gate.

MOSHE
(Surprised)
The other side of the fence?

SHLOMO
Just a little ways from the gate.

MOSHE
The other side— That's hard, Shlomo.

SHLOMO
Have you forgotten! How I helped you when I was barracks clerk?

MOSHE
No. But the other side. That's hard.

SHLOMO
(Unconvincingly)
I won't be on the bottom for long.

Moshe looks down at the tiny piece of bread resting in his cupped hand. He sighs and then looks up, smiling reassuringly.

MOSHE
I'll try.

Scene 20

Rubin, standing by the latrine, watches Abie approaching Miska at the gravel mound as smoke rises from the chimney.

ABIE
Ready?

MISKA
No. My Father said no.

ABIE

Too bad, kid.

Abie walks away from the gravel mound going toward the latrine and walks up to Rubin.

No deal.

RUBIN

That little shit!

ABIE

Let it go.

RUBIN

I'll break 'im into a hundred pieces.

ABIE

It's too dangerous. The SS are all over the place and if Moll—

RUBIN

I just hate letting 'em have it.
   (Rubin turns toward the chimney)
Sooner or later, we'll all be ashes. Ah . . . Maybe you're right. That little shit!

Four prisoners are passing the latrine, pulling and pushing a heavy cart loaded with gravel. The cart stops near the mound. Rubin turns to Abie who stands there, stunned.

ABIE

See that old man by the corner of the gravel cart?

Rubin looks, and then turns back to Abie.

RUBIN

You know 'im?

ABIE

Discreetly, send him over here. And keep the cart there 'til I finish with him.
   (Rubin stares at Abie)
It's my father.

Rubin nods and walks toward the gravel mound.

RUBIN

   (Shouts)
You! By the cart!

The prisoners by the cart anxiously look at the Kapo. Rubin points to Abie's Father.

Now! While you can still walk!

Abie's Father cautiously approaches. Rubin grabs his shirt.

So, you like keeping the Kapo waiting!

Raising his hand implying an impending blow, Rubin turns him toward the latrine.

   (Softly)
Go to the latrine. Your son's there.
   (Rubin shoves him)
Move!

Abie's Father hurries to the latrine, as the gravel mound fades into a half-light and the cart moves off stage.

ABIE

Over here, Dad.

Abie's Father peeks around the corner.

ABIE'S FATHER

Avraham?

ABIE

(To himself)
I ate half-rations for five days.

Abie's Father joins his son.

ABIE'S FATHER

Avraham.

ABIE

The letter. I had a letter smuggled out.

ABIE'S FATHER

Your letter?

ABIE

Didn't you get my letter?

ABIE'S FATHER

(Anxious)
We brought it with us. Everything was taken when we arrived.

ABIE

But I told— I told you! Take Mama and the girls and little Yankel— Leave Hungary! Or at least, hide!

ABIE'S FATHER
We did. Well, we tried. But it happened so fast.

ABIE
(Reluctance compounded with a dreaded anxiety)
Did . . . everyone come?

ABIE'S FATHER
The others are somewhere.

Abie glares at his Father as his left hand forms into a fist.

When we arrived, I went one way— they went another.

Abie begins slowly tapping his leg in an uneven, halting motion with his fist.

Hymie Dorfman. You know, the egg man. Kept changing his offer for the business.
   (Expressing astonishment with open hands and raised shoulders)
I couldn't give it away! So we haggled, day in, day out. Always the same with Hymie; he plays the fool, but he's smart as a fox.
   (With a slight smile, he nods, making a clicking sound)
But I was on to him.

ABIE
Dad! . . . lat— later.
   (Shaking his head)
Can't . . . can't talk.

Abie's Father is surprised.

It's too dangerous to talk here. You should return to your cart.

                        ABIE'S FATHER
When will I see you again, Avraham?

                        ABIE
Soon. You should go now.

Abie's Father slowly nods and leaves as Abie watches. The gravel mound returns to full light as Abie's Father rejoins the prisoners by the cart, which is now empty. Rubin picks up a small rock, flinging it at them.

                        RUBIN
Why are you still here?

The prisoners begin moving the cart. Abie raises his fist, biting down on it as he leans against the latrine wall, watching his Father moving across the stage. When the cart is gone, Abie turns toward Miska and Miska's Father at the gravel mound. His expression changes, becoming hardened and calculating as he lowers his arm to his side, clenching the other hand into a fist. Janko leaves his wheelbarrow and quickly moves up to Miska.

                        JANKO
Have they said anything?

Miska glances at the Kapo and then turns to his Father, shaking his head. Abie's lower arms start to quiver with a controlled anger. Janko returns to his wheelbarrow as Abie begins walking toward the gravel mound. He stops before reaching it.

                        ABIE
Kapo.
   (Rubin joins him)
The way to get your crown is through the father.

Rubin's eyes light up.

                    RUBIN

I must be getting rusty.
   (Shouts)
Sergi!

                    SERGI

Yes, Kapo.

                    RUBIN

Come here!

Scene 21

At the trench, Primo II bends down and pantomimes filling his shovel as Izak approaches wearing his new shoes. Primo II turns to deposit the imaginary dirt by Shlomo and notices Izak, standing above Shlomo, shining his shoe against his pant leg. Izak glances into the trench to see how much progress has been made, but he really doesn't care. He then stares at the prisoner leaving the trench with the wheelbarrow that Nachman has just filled. Meanwhile, Shlomo, lost in his own thoughts, automatically lifts his shovel and without looking, pantomimes throwing the dirt out of the trench. Izak reacts to the imaginary dirt hitting his pants and falling on his new shoes. He raises each leg, shaking one shoe and then the other. Seething with anger, he looks down into the trench at Shlomo.

                    IZAK

   (Shouts)
You!

Shlomo turns, looking up to Izak.

Get your ass down to the end.

Shlomo snaps out of his daze.

                    SHLOMO
What?

Instantly, Izak pantomimes kicking dirt into Shlomo's face, momentarily blinding him. Letting go of his shovel, Shlomo covers his eyes, trying to clear the dirt away. Izak grabs Nachman's shovel, whacking Shlomo on the side of the head with the flat end.

                    IZAK
(Shouts)
Now!

Shlomo staggers toward the deep end of the trench dragging his shovel. He reaches over to tap Leib's shoulder, but instead hits him on the back of the head, knocking off his glasses.

                    LEIB
Huh?

Leib immediately turns around and inadvertently steps on his glasses.

                    SHLOMO
(Spoken in an injured/guttural tone)
Move!

Leib picks up his glasses and takes a couple of steps. He holds up the glasses, staring at the damage as Shlomo moves in front of him. Leib shakes his head while he straightens the frame. Putting on his glasses, Leib covers the good lens as he struggles to focus through the cracked lens.

                    IZAK
Marker.

Leib lowers his hand, looking up at Izak, who points to the middle of the trench. Leib grabs his shovel and moves. Izak stares at Shlomo for a few moments, and then leaves in disgust.

Scene 22

On the platform, the prisoners are working on the rail bed laying the track. Tomasz is sitting next to the track while two prisoners stand nearby him. One is holding several splice plates while the other is holding a large wrench. Tomasz raises his hand.

TOMASZ

Splice plate.

It is put into his hand. He places it on the outside of the rail, overlapping the joint.

Splice plate.

He reaches up for another one and places it on the inside, lining up the holes. Again, he raises his open hand.

Bolts.
   (Nothing happens. After a moment, he yells louder)
Bolts!

Alberto runs over with a box of bolts.

ALBERTO

How many?

TOMASZ

(Frustrated)
Two!
(Recognizing Alberto, he smiles)
There are always two for each set of plates.

Alberto nods, handing him the bolts. Tomasz hand-tightens the bolts, and then tells Alberto.

Give him the bolts and take the wrench.

Holding the wrench, Alberto sits opposite Tomasz. They secure the bolts.

Good.

They stand up as Tomasz looks toward Feliks, who is working down the rail bed on the other track, and nods.

Has he been to see you?

Alberto shakes his head. Feliks, holding a large wrench, shouts at his helper.

FELIKS

Hold the wrench steady!

The frail prisoner, a Tailor sitting opposite Feliks, applies more pressure to his wrench. They finish tightening the bolts.

What were you, Jew, before you became a rail layer? Huh! A doctor or a lawyer?

TAILOR

Tailor. I made the finest clothes in Poznan.

Feliks smiles, pulling at his shirt.

FELIKS
Now they're no better than mine, huh, Jew?

TOMASZ
(Shouts)
Feliks! Come here!
(Turning to the two prisoners who work with him and Alberto)
Move! Down the track.

The two prisoners walk away. Feliks walks up and, recognizing Alberto, he frowns.

You have something for him?

Feliks reaches inside his shirt to the hidden pocket and reluctantly hands Alberto the apple slice.

Let's keep working.

Feliks leaves as Alberto raises his closed hand, smelling the apple's fragrance.

My way of saying thanks.

Alberto slips the apple slice into the hidden pocket inside his shirt.

ALBERTO
I have a favor to ask.

TOMASZ
What!

ALBERTO
I have a comrade working on the other side of the fence. He wants over to this side.

Tomasz looks toward the unseen guard in the distance.

TOMASZ
I heard about that guard . . . your comrade, he's from Buna?

ALBERTO
Yes.

TOMASZ
Then he can work on any squad. If you can get him over to this side, I'll make the switch.

ALBERTO
How?

TOMASZ
The latrine chaperone.

Alberto nods and they begin walking to the next rail joint.

Scene 23

Standing by the gravel mound, Miska is filling his father's wheelbarrow.

MISKA
I'll take my time.

Janko nods, casually standing there as Sergi approaches.

SERGI
More!

Janko quickly lifts the wheelbarrow's handles as Sergi stands in front of it, glaring at Miska.

I'll tell you when to stop.
  (Pointing to the wheelbarrow)
More!

Miska continues filling the wheelbarrow at a faster pace.

Stop!
  (Turning to Janko)
Let's go.

Janko has difficulty controlling his overfilled wheelbarrow. He leaves the gravel mound, with Sergi at his side. Using his truncheon, Sergi redirects him.

We'll take a shortcut through the field! Faster! You lazy pig!

Suddenly, Janko's wheelbarrow hits a rut, stopping abruptly. The wheelbarrow tips over as Janko lands on the ground. Sergi pokes him with the truncheon.

Up! Get up!

A dazed Janko slowly stands up. At the gravel mound Miska stops filling the wheelbarrow in front of him and looks toward his Father. The prisoner, whose wheelbarrow is being filled waits nervously as he notices Kapo Rubin approaching. Sergi again prods Janko with his truncheon.

Don't just stand there! Fix your wheelbarrow.

Janko rights the wheelbarrow.

Well?

Janko stares at him.

Fill it!

Kneeling, Janko lifts a handful of small rocks into the wheelbarrow. Sergi looks back to the gravel mound, making sure that Miska is observing them. The waiting prisoner looks at Rubin who indicates with a hand motion "it's all right." Sergi, satisfied that he has Miska's attention, shouts at Janko loud enough for Miska to hear.

You shit! Trying to make me look bad? Pick 'em up with your teeth!

Again, Janko stares at Sergi.

Did you hear me!
 (Screams)
NOW!

Janko freezes. Sergi explodes, swinging the truncheon against the wheelbarrow, causing a shattering sound. Instantly, Janko drops down on all fours. He moves slowly with a deliberate, mechanical movement, picking up a rock with his teeth. Moving to the wheelbarrow, he raises his hands, grabbing its rim. Lifting his head to the center of the barrow, he drops the rock. His body goes limp except for his arms that stiffen as his grip tightens on the rim. His arms begin trembling, shaking the wheelbarrow uncontrollably.

MISKA

 (Shouts)
Stop! Stop it!

He turns to Rubin while Janko and Sergi fade into darkness as the sound of the wheelbarrow, rocking back and forth, continues.

You can have it. Only, stop it!

RUBIN

Kept me waiting! That will cost ya. You can forget the rations, kid.

Darkness, as the sound of the rocking wheelbarrow continues. Beat, beat, beat.

Scene 24

In the dim light of the latrine, a prisoner sits on a commode as Moshe waits near the entrance. Alberto walks in. He pauses for a moment analyzing the situation as his eyes adjust to the light. He moves next to Moshe.

ALBERTO

I need a prisoner brought from the other side of the fence to the latrine.

MOSHE

Dangerous.

ALBERTO

I understand.

Alberto nudges Moshe, signaling him to turn around, facing away from the prisoner on the commode. Alberto places the apple quarter in Moshe's hand. Pleasantly surprised, Moshe smiles and then tries hiding his enthusiasm.

MOSHE

I have to bring another prisoner first.

ALBERTO

My prisoner first.

Moshe raises his closed fist, smelling the fruit.

MOSHE
Who, Italian? Your comrade?

Alberto nods.

Scene 25

Shlomo is digging at the deep end of the trench while Primo II is working near the middle. Leaning on his shovel, Nachman watches Moshe approaching.

MOSHE
(Shouts)
Latrine chaperone.

Nachman acknowledges Moshe with a nod. Shlomo lets go of his shovel, turns around and starts moving out of the trench. He's next to Primo II but doesn't notice that Primo II also begins leaving the trench. Standing on the rim with a guilty expression, Moshe looks down at Shlomo.

Shlomo, he's first. I'll come back for you.

Shlomo, continuing to walk out, glances toward Moshe with a puzzled look. Moshe places his hand on Shlomo's shoulder, stopping him.

Shlomo.
(Nods towards Primo II)
He's first!

Shlomo looks at Primo II as he slips by him. He grabs Primo II's arm.

SHLOMO
I won't forget this!

Primo II pulls away. Shlomo turns to Moshe and stares at him with a child-like expression of "why?"

MOSHE

I'll be back soon!

Glaring at Moshe for a moment, Shlomo moves back to the deep end of the trench as the other prisoners fade into darkness. He moves his shovel in a slow, deliberate fashion, pantomiming picking up a small amount of dirt and depositing it behind him. He turns back to the wall as his Mother is heard singing a Yiddish lullaby. Staring at the dirt wall in front of him, Shlomo searches the various shreds of his earliest memories. He reaches out to the wall, as if trying to touch those memories. Shlomo's Mother is illuminated on the other side of the wall as Shlomo fades into a shadowy half-light. She hums as she leans over the crib, gently tucking in her son's blanket. When she's done, she stops humming, smiling at the sleeping baby.

SHLOMO'S MOTHER

My son. My lovely little son. There are so many things we can't give you, but you are healthy and, oh, so beautiful!

The light slowly brightens, illuminating the prisoners in the trench as it correspondingly fades on Shlomo's Mother.

My little wonder. My sweet, sweet child. You will have a better life. Sleep, my precious. My little bundle of joy.

The forlorn prisoners in the trench continue digging as Shlomo's Mother, unseen in darkness, is heard speaking to the rhythm of the shovels.

  (Off stage)
A better life . . .
  (Slowly fading out)
A better life . . . my son.

Scene 26

Kapo Rubin and the Dentist enter the dimly lit latrine and wait for their eyes to adjust. In the shadows, sitting on the commodes, Abie calmly waits with Miska, who stares at them with fearful eyes.

DENTIST
But what will I use?

Rubin hands him a makeshift camp knife.

This?

RUBIN
You have a problem?

Scene 27

The Yiddish lullaby is heard as the dimly-lit platform begins to brighten, awash in the unifying glow of warm hues and soft tones. The prisoners working on the track are performing their different tasks. A prisoner wipes his brow, another sets the proper alignment of a rail as he gently taps it with his pick; others concentrate on tightening bolts or pounding spikes into the ties, securing the rails. They are working in harmony, oblivious to their circumstance and absorbed in their endeavor. For several minutes they move in unison as a visual dance cascading across the platform. Suddenly, a scream emanates from the highlighted latrine, obliterating the lullaby. The warm hues abruptly transition into a harsh, linear illumination, accentuating the individual prisoners. Instantly, they move in a disjointed, haphazard manner, stoically performing their tasks. The light begins to dim on the platform as Miska stumbles out of the latrine. Kapo Rubin follows, quickly catching up with him as the platform becomes dark. Physically supporting Miska in a subtle way, Rubin tries to conceal his condition as they walk across the stage.

RUBIN

Walk straight, kid. Can't attract any attention or it will go badly for both of us. I'll make sure you have it easy, till you leave for Buna.

Scene 28

Several prisoners are emptying the bodies from the wagon onto the platform. Two prisoners pick up a body and carry it toward the center of the platform. They swing the body, back and forth, throwing it into the pit. Bordering the pit are stacks of wood. Rubin, supporting Miska, crosses the stage to Janko, who stands near a pile of broken wheelbarrows, staring at the bodies being thrown into the pit.

RUBIN

You'll work on these, till you leave for Buna.

Rubin walks away as Janko stares at Miska for a moment. Then he reaches up, tenderly touching Miska's swollen cheek.

MISKA

I'm . . . all right.

He staggers a little as Janko grabs him and continues to hold him.

Now, there's nothing . . . nothing more, they can take from us.

Janko looks at his son with a sad, troubled smile and nods reassuringly. Then he looks as another body is thrown into the pit.

Scene 29

At the trench, Shlomo (dancer) digs as the Yiddish lullaby is hummed. Listening to the melody, Shlomo stops digging.

SHLOMO-DANCER
(Spoken in the voice of a frightened, shivering child)
Mama . . . it's dark . . . coooold.

Touching the dirt wall in front of him.

I'm scared, Mama!

Lena is heard giggling and the humming abruptly ends.

Mama? Lena?
(Returning to normal voice)
Lena, is that you?

Lena, wearing a nightgown, is illuminated on the other side of the trench wall. She reaches out as if to touch the dancer's hand.

LENA
C'mon . . .

The trench goes dark as Lena rotates onto the bed where Shlomo is sleeping. She nudges his shoulder.

You have to get up. You'll be late for work.

SHLOMO
I don't care.

LENA

(Sing-song voice)
Sh-lo-mo.

SHLOMO

I can't move.

LENA

Your father will be mad.

SHLOMO

He's always mad.

LENA

He'll yell at you again!

SHLOMO

Eh!

Shlomo stretches as Lena mimics her father-in-law's voice.

LENA

I don't understand. The honeymoon's over. Shlomo! Get serious.

Shlomo raises his head, holding it up in the palm of his hand, his elbow resting on the mattress.

SHLOMO

Yeah. Get serious. Give me some grandchildren!

LENA

He doesn't say that.

SHLOMO

Ah! Lena. Lena. I don't ever want to leave you.

LENA
A while ago, you left me for the bathroom.

SHLOMO
I'm serious.

LENA
Such a serious man I married.

Shlomo sits up.

SHLOMO
When we're together—

LENA
You're blushing.

SHLOMO
Lena.

LENA
I love it when you blush. You look so cute.

SHLOMO
(Annoyed)
Lena! Let me finish.

LENA
Sorry.

SHLOMO
There are moments. Moments. When we're together . . .

Brushing back a lock of her hair.

That I feel, I—

Softly, Lena presses her finger against his lips.

LENA

Shh . . . For me too.
  (Slowly fade into darkness)
For me too.

In the transition just before the next scene opens.

IZAK

  (Shouts from off stage)
Everyone out! Everyone out!
  (Pause. Normal voice as a warning)
Kapo's coming!

Scene 30

In the dim light of the platform the large wagon stands empty, while nearby a few bodies wait for the pit. The barbed wire fence cuts diagonally across the stage, from its narrowest point on the platform where the Guard Otto is observing the prisoners, to its widest point down stage. Moving slowly, the trench prisoners enter from the side of the stage, carrying their shovels. Leaving the group, Shlomo moves down the fence line, standing alone, staring through the barbed wire. The other prisoners cluster together, looking upstage at the shadowy prisoners on the platform who are throwing another body into the pit.

JOSHUA

What are they doing?

Leib joins Joshua. He takes his glasses off. Fogging the good lens, he begins rubbing it with his prison shirt while looking toward the prisoners throwing another body into the pit.

NACHMAN
They're doing their job. Just like us. Digging a hole— filling a hole— till supper and a warm bowl of soup.

LEIB
Are those . . . bodies?

Leib puts his glasses on.

GREEK
That's where . . . our women end up, our children, our parents—

JOSHUA
They went to another camp.

GREEK
That's where we will end up.

Leib looks on in shock but doesn't speak.

JOSHUA
How can you be sure?

NACHMAN
He doesn't understand.

GREEK
He doesn't *want* to understand.

Joshua turns away in anguish. Kapo Rubin grabs Leib's arm.

RUBIN

Time to measure.

Leib follows Rubin off stage. The platform brightens as Captain Moll enters walking toward the pit. The Captain watches the prisoners swing the last body back and forth, and then release it. Shlomo lets go of his shovel and reaches out, as if trying to grasp the fleeting body. The Guard Otto raises his rifle.

OTTO

Verboten!

CAPTAIN MOLL

Fire the pits!

Instantly, the platform darkens as flames erupt covering the back wall of the stage. Shlomo's extended hand forms into a fist.

SHLOMO

(Screams)
LEEE-NAAH!

The sound of a shot. Shlomo collapses, lying still on the stage. The Guard and Rubin come running up to Shlomo's body.

OTTO

(Shouts)
Prisoner! Attempting to escape!

RUBIN

He's climbing into the camp!

The Guard nudges Shlomo, using the barrel of his rifle and his boot, confirming he's dead. Satisfied, he turns to Rubin.

OTTO
(Slow and threatening)
Attempting to escape.

Rubin grabs the two closest prisoners, motioning toward the body.

RUBIN
Pick 'im up! Let this be a lesson to anyone who's thinking of escaping. Izak!

The guard smiles.

Scene 31

Primo I is highlighted as he walks out from the side of the dark stage. Setting his briefcase down, he waits.

TEACHER
(Off stage)
Class, Mr. Levi has come here today to tell us about his experiences in a concentration camp during the war.

Primo I steps forward to address the class while the stage remains dark.

PRIMO I
I was twenty-four, naive and inexperienced. Attempting to be a partisan, I went to the mountains with a group of friends. We were there but a short time when three fascist militia companies stumbled onto our refuge and captured us. During my interrogation, I felt that death was imminent and decided to admit my status as an Italian citizen, "of Jewish race." As a Jew, I was sent to a detention camp at Fossoli, near Modena; it was January, 1944. Eventually, there were over six hundred and fifty men,

women, and children, all "of Jewish race," waiting for deportation. To where? We did not know.

Standing still at center stage next to the platform, the prisoners, including Primo II, are slowly emerging out of the darkness into a shadowy half-light, looking bewildered, confused, and shocked.

But on February 21st a train arrived with twelve empty wagons. Everyone knew this was one of those notorious transport trains, "the kind that never return." We boarded that morning and waited until evening before departing.

Highlighted, the prisoners step forward, individually and in small groups, becoming a formation marching in place.

We had entered a void, separated from the world in the darkness of our cramped, sealed compartment. We were not among the living, though we were alive. We were not yet dead, but death was waiting for us. Time. Time had no meaning except for the thirst that tormented our bodies or the cold that teased us into numbness. The train began moving.

Primo I begins fading into a half-light as the prisoners' cadence and physical stature wanes with each step.

On and on, endlessly, the wheels creaked along the track in a journey to nothingness. Where the more fortunate, upon their arrival, would be ushered into a welcoming chamber and suffocated with Zyklon B gas.

A Kapo walks out and just his presence, without speaking, commands the prisoners to do a right face and march off the stage as it darkens. The prisoners enter the platform in a half-light, slowly marching behind the barbed wire fence toward the chimney.

And the few of us that remained would walk into the twilight world of the camps where we immediately sank to the bottom. We'd rot in the rain, shiver in the wind, and march in an endless sea of mud. Soon, very soon, we became unrecognizable, even to ourselves.

Crossing the platform, the formation begins losing its rhythm as each prisoner starts moving in his own debilitating style, but still as a unit.

We are the inhabitants of this gray world where, with each step, we feel our lives receding.

Primo II steps out of the formation and goes up to the fence. He stares in the direction of Primo I with a weary gaze. Very slowly, the stage brightens as Primo I pantomimes his lecture while the formation continues across the platform. Before reaching the end of the platform, the prisoners disappear into darkness as the crematory chimney glows a rose color. Primo I continues pantomiming the lecture until the last marching prisoner is gone. He then stands still waiting.

TEACHER
(Off stage)
Before Mr. Levi leaves, are there any questions you would like to ask him? . . . Alfonso.

Primo II is highlighted, still looking through the barbed wire.

ALFONSO
(Off stage)
Why didn't you escape?

Primo I becomes despondent and turns toward Primo II. They stare at each other for a moment. Primo II turns around and walks across the width of the platform as it darkens. After a moment, Primo I walks over and picks up his briefcase as Shlomo appears at his side.

SHLOMO

Did you really think they'd understand? The books— the awards— what does it all mean? . . . Only those who were there can understand.

They start walking.

Scene 32

Primo I and Shlomo cross the stage as a line of people enter the front door of the bus at the side of the stage.

SHLOMO

You talk of gas chambers and crematories. They worry about the right bus fare.

Primo I, with a faraway, dazed look, stops at the center of the stage and stares at the people. As the people enter the bus, they go off stage and instantly return as prisoners in a formation. The formation begins marching near the platform as it slowly moves across the stage. The faint sound of the camp's orchestra fades in and the bus disappears into darkness.

PRISONER I

We're near Buna. Hear the music?

PRISONER II

They must be marching in.

PRISONER I

Why are we slowing down?

PRISONER II

Looks like they're stopping up front!

PRISONER III
What for?

PRISONER II
Who knows?

PRISONER I
Kapo!

BUNA KAPO
(Shouts)
Column, halt!

The formation stops.

Left face!

The prisoners face the platform as the Kapo counts the ranks. The sound of approaching army transport trucks fades in.

PRISONER III
Transports! They're taking us to the gas!

PRISONER I
Shut up!

The sound of women screaming. A group of dancers, wearing light beige, skin-colored leotards, are illuminated in a half-light. They slowly move as shadows across the platform as if confined to the back of a military truck.

PRISONER III
They're liquidating the women's camp!

HUNGARIAN PRISONER
Liquidate! What does that mean?

PRISONER I

Shut up!

BUNA KAPO

(Shouts)
Quiet! You pigs!

The Kapo delivers blows, subduing the prisoners. Now there is an eerie silence as the prisoners stand, lifelessly, staring at the women. The light brightens on the platform as the women now notice the prisoners in their silent formation. Lena takes a step backwards glancing at Shlomo, but still moving at the same pace as the other women.

WOMEN

(Shouting as they reach out)
Save us! Help us! Don't let them do this! Help us! We're going to the gas!

Lena looks at the formation.

LENA

(Shouts)
Prisoners! Remember!

SHLOMO

Lena?

LENA

(Shouts)
Remember what they did here! And tell the world! Tell them!
(Spoken in a low register with an "other-worldly" quality)
What you have seen!

The women fade into darkness as the motorized sound of the trucks fades off.

SHLOMO
(Softly to himself with finality)
Lena.

Unable to move, Shlomo watches the prisoners do a right face and silently march off the stage as Primo I starts walking. Shlomo turns toward Primo I with a sympathetic look. He reaches out to grasp Primo I's arm, but Primo I is beyond his reach. Shlomo joins the formation of prisoners leaving the stage. Noticing that Shlomo isn't beside him, Primo I stops. He turns, looking back at the empty stage where Shlomo stood. After a moment, he turns back and continues walking.

Scene 33

The dancer playing Primo I opens an imaginary door and enters the apartment house lobby. He goes to the high staircase. Standing there, he looks up at what he perceives is a formidable challenge. He then grabs the railing with one hand while still holding his briefcase in the other and begins climbing. Slowly, step by step, he pulls himself up as the railway foreman, Tomasz, faces upstage.

TOMASZ
(Shouts)
Prisoners!

The prisoners are illuminated, bracing themselves as they grab the turntable. Nearby is a rail car filled with ashes. Kapo Borslaw is waiting impatiently in his soggy poncho near the rail car as two prisoners are ready to push the car onto the turntable.

(Shouts)
Up!

The prisoners slowly raise the turntable, rotating it to meet the rail car filled with ashes.

Down!

The two prisoners push the rail car onto the turntable. They join the other prisoners around the turntable as Borslaw walks over to Tomasz.

BORSLAW
These ponchos are worthless!

Tomasz is soaked to the bone.

TOMASZ
It is wet, Kapo.

BORSLAW
(Shouts)
Are you ready, railway foreman?

TOMASZ
(Shouts)
Yes, Kapo!

BORSLAW
Good. Because the cremos are overflowing.

Primo I stops on the first landing, resting.

Well, what are you waiting for?

TOMASZ
(Shouts)
Prisoners! Up!

Primo I starts the next flight as the prisoners bend down, grip the turntable, and try lifting it, but the extra weight of the rail car makes it too heavy. Tomasz raises his arms like an orchestra conductor.

  (Shouts)
Prisoners! Up!

Again, the turntable doesn't move. One of the prisoners, unable to stay on his feet, slips and falls next to the turntable.

TURNTABLE PRISONER I

  (Muttering)
Too heavy! Too heavy!

Several of the prisoners run over, kicking him.

TURNTABLE PRISONER II

  (Shouts)
Move, you slacker!

TURNTABLE PRISONER III

  (Shouts)
You worthless shit! Get up!

TURNTABLE PRISONER I

  (Muttering)
It's too heavy! Too heavy, comrades!

Turntable Prisoner IV pushes the other prisoners away as he stands over the fallen prisoner giving him a chance to stand up, yelling into his face.

TURNTABLE PRISONER IV

Get up! Up!
  (Eyeing the Kapo)
Hurry.

Using all his strength, the prisoner lifts himself up and stands next to the turntable as the others get into position. Seeing this prisoner standing there, Borslaw runs up.

> BORSLAW
> *(Shouts)*
> You dogs! Can't you do anything without my help?

Delivering another blow to the battered prisoner.

Again, railway foreman!

> TOMASZ
> *(Shouts)*
> Prisoners! Up!

Borslaw picks up a stick, delivering "blows of encouragement" to the straining prisoners.

Up!

In chorus, the prisoners shout out with fear.

> PRISONERS

Up!

The turntable doesn't move as Borslaw circles the prisoners swinging the stick. Tomasz runs to the turntable and bends down gripping it as the prisoners scream in desperation.

Up!

The prisoners slowly lift the turntable and rotate it.

TOMASZ
(Shouts)
Down!

Borslaw walks to where the turntable's track meets the other rails.

BORSLAW
(Shouts)
Hurry!

The stage darkens; the turntable, prisoners, and rail car disappear, while Primo I is still seen climbing the stairs. A second rail car appears on the platform, filled with ashes and illuminated by a strobe light. The light flickers to the sound of the car rolling over the rail joints. The faster the strobe light flickers, the slower Primo I climbs. He lets go of his briefcase, it tumbles down the stairs as he grabs the railing with both hands, pulling. The rail car disappears as the image of ashes, falling endlessly, covers the back wall of the stage. Primo I stares at the ashes, spellbound by the constant flow as he stands motionless on the stairs. Alberto appears behind Primo I, reaching out, touching Primo I's shoulder.

ALBERTO
It's time, Primo.

Primo I quickly turns around.

PRIMO I
Alberto?

Instantly, Alberto and the ashes disappear. Primo I tumbles down the stairs illuminated by the flickering of a strobe light. The stage darkens before Primo I reaches the bottom.

Scene 34

Dazed and exhausted men, women, and children dressed in everyday clothes, enter the platform. Moving through Auschwitz's front gate, they continue crossing the platform. Entering the stage, wearing skin-colored leotards, they drift aimlessly around the large space, lost in confusion and curiosity as the platform darkens. They pass Primo I, center stage near the platform, sitting at his desk writing, unaware of their presence.

The sound of a metal door slamming shut echoes across the stage. Spreading a cold, piercing fear ricocheting off the concrete, some stop immediately, others quiver uncontrollably, a few frantically jerk their heads in every direction, searching. Suddenly, in unison, everyone looks up, staring at the ceiling as they make a high-pitched, hissing sound. Despondent and somber, they move in a slow, almost enigmatic trance, periodically punctuated by the suffocating agony of a few individuals while they succumb to the gas.

Collapsing to the stage, they expose Primo I, who is holding up a page contemplating its words. After a moment he places the page face down on top of the stack of papers. Turning the stack over he moves it to the center of the desk. For a few moments, he stares at the manuscript with a contented glow, and then gently taps it.

Instantly, the bodies become animated, as if awakened from a dream. They rise up merging into a group, obscuring Primo I and his desk and chair, disappearing under the platform. Moving down stage, they wait until the shadowy image of the crematory chimney appears on the dark platform. Turning around, they begin singing "pree" in a low monotone while moving toward the platform. At the platform they sing out "mo" in a rising pitch as they turn their heads upwards toward the chimney. Slowly they raise their arms, as if guiding Primo I towards the chimney with their hands.

The stage darkens and the dancers disappear while a faint light appears at the bottom center of the chimney. The light slowly rises, brightening as it moves up the chimney to the sound of a solo woodwind instrument playing a delicate, ethereal melody. Reaching the top, the light vanishes.

Instantly, dimly lit shapes emerge at the back of the platform. Slowly the light begins to brighten, revealing a group wearing white luminous leotards covered by loose fitting, white sheer outer garments. A dark shape begins to rise up from a kneeling position at the front of the platform, standing silhouetted against the luminous images. The glowing images create a circle with an opening toward the distant, dark figure in front of them.

A seductive, high-pitched solo voice emanates from the forming circle, enticing the shadowy figure. He moves toward the light, becoming recognizable as a man dressed in light beige leotards that are covered with specks of a white luminous material. The circle glows brighter as the others join in the alluring song while reaching out with their raised arms, beckoning the approaching individual.

Moving closer to the circle, the light transforms the beige leotards into a brilliant white. A slight breeze blows as the outer garments of the angelic images flutter in the wind. Primo I enters the circle and it begins closing around him as the singing grows fainter and fainter. Disappearing in the celestial embrace, silence spreads over the platform as the breeze intensifies while the circle glows brighter in its radiance. Beat, beat, beat, beat. Darkness!

END OF PLAY

EPILOGUE

EPILOGUE

A few months before my tenth birthday the Korean War ended. There was a sense of relief in the air that even I could recognize. I wondered how an event so far away could affect the people around me. Maybe the world was larger than I believed, stranger than I realized, closer than I thought? My life seemed unchanged; every day moved to the same rhythmic beat, surrounding me in the warmth and comfort of childhood. But now I began observing in broader strokes, with a keener insight.

These are the impressionable years, when religious and cultural institutions are determined to influence the young minds within their purview by shaping and structuring their identity.

I started preparing for my Bar Mitzvah, a religious ceremony that would signify, in the context of Jewish culture, my attainment of manhood at age thirteen. This required attending class twice a week after school to learn how to pronounce Hebrew to read prayers and participate in religious ceremonies. There was also an emphasis on attending Saturday morning Sabbath services at the synagogue.

Every Saturday morning, dressed in my suit, I walked to the synagogue. I walked along the busy residential avenue, stopping at the light. While waiting, I would glance across the street, past the parochial school, to the impressive large, gray-stone Catholic church in the middle of the block. That side of the street ran to the Parkway with its large, grass-covered median with trees running down the middle.

I walked up a short, steep hill and crossed to a secluded street tucked in between the busy avenue and the park. Canterbury Street was special. All the houses were single family homes bordered by landscaping and trees. It was a quiet street, a totally different ambience than I was accustomed to. It was only a few blocks from my house, yet so different. My street was made up of crowded houses containing two flats, surrounded by blocks and blocks of the same construction.

Every Saturday during the three years I went to the synagogue I walked down the same side of Canterbury Street. I don't recall ever seeing other people there, though there may have been. The mystique of that street created an illusion that transported me to another place. I called the street "Europe." This was not the Europe of fairy tales and castles. It was the Europe of art and culture, which I knew nothing about. It was where we came from, even if we usually represented the underclass. Though there was an ocean between us, we seemed inseparable. America was an extension of that world, young and exciting, but not yet finished or formed.

Walking down the gentle slope in the peaceful solitude of the moment, I became lost in my imagination. The visual surroundings seemed to merge into the sensory feelings of warm hues and faint vibrations, bringing the semblance of an enigmatic past. An incomprehensible experience, which I accepted and even relished, evaporated when reaching the Parkway.

Turning the corner, I continued past the high school, a large, white-stone building that occupied the entire block, four stories high. Even at that age I related to this building in a special way. This was where my mother and uncle had gone to high school, and where he now taught Latin and other foreign languages. It would eventually become the high school that my brother and I would attend, and where he would graduate as valedictorian.

I continued a short distance until I reached my synagogue. I entered through a side door to where the Bar Mitzvah students met. A teacher instructed us on the religious reading of the week, which the rabbi usually elaborated on in his sermon. At the appropriate time we were led upstairs into the sanctuary.

There were three sections of pews, one section on each side under the balconies where the women sat, and a center section in front of the bimah, a raised platform surrounded by a marble balustrade.

EPILOGUE

In the center of the bimah was a table for the Torah scrolls (the five books of Moses) to be rolled out and read. There were two chairs on the bimah, placed against the back wall with the ark between them, one for the rabbi and the other for the cantor. Above the ark which held the Torah scrolls was a replica of the Ten Commandments lit by the soft glow of the hanging eternal light. The first two rows in the center section were reserved for the Bar Mitzvah students.

There was a rhythm and structure to the service that was either read, chanted, or sung in Hebrew. Only the rabbi's sermon was in English. In the beginning, I found this new experience intriguing and exciting, but as it became familiar and I started participating, it moved into the realm of magical. The Hebrew words, unintelligible to me, melted into the melody, enveloping me in a world of melodic sounds. I sang and swayed, immersed in the sweet euphoria of the moment, never questioning or seeking a meaning, satisfied only by the joy of singing and chanting.

In every service the rabbi delivered a sermon. Each one held my interest and usually related to the Torah reading of the week. Sometimes, when speaking about one of the prophets, his sermon would soar. I sat there listening intently, in awe of God's power as his prophesies always became a reality in ancient times. But the most penetrating, compelling sermons that touched me every time were the ones on the Holocaust, which had a transformative power that lingered beyond the presence of the sanctuary.

Looking back, I now realize that the research and documentation of the death camps was beginning to be published at this time. The initial shock American Jews experienced at the end of the war was compounded by this new information. Their anguish was raw, cutting. The rabbi's sermon wasn't abstract like a passage from the Torah, or moralistic on how we should live our lives. It was the unimaginable; reverberating screams and tormenting visions ending in darkness, silence. It was where my people, the Ashkenazi Jews, disappeared.

The service ended with the usual uplifting songs. The congregants greeted each other, wishing a "Good Sabbath," and then celebrated with a little wine and a slice of cake. I always felt that the Saturday morning service represented an American interpretation of the world the immigrants had left behind.

Leaving the synagogue, I began retracing my steps. Enjoying the fresh air, feeling invigorated, I always looked forward to my walk home. The buildings and houses sparkled in the afternoon sun, reflecting the future's alluring glow that was America at this time. I was only a kid, not happy or sad, just impatient to grow up.

Entering Canterbury Street I moved up the gentle slope, soaking in the beauty that surrounded me. I began to feel a slight aching coming from a faraway, obscure place, yet inside me. This peculiar stirring, this vague sensation was internal, deep, beyond my comprehension. It started moving, rising, intensifying, swirling, surging higher and higher. The light began fading, breathing was harder— still rising, spreading, all consuming until my entire body screamed:

"Germany! *Germany!* I forgive you!
For to hate you . . . is to be like you."

Not a sound passed my lips. My chest heaved, gulping the afternoon air as the tear, rolling down my check, warmed in the sun. Fragments of colors slowly emerged, coalescing into images of houses and trees. My body momentarily quivered, though my pace never lost a beat. The sun brightened as I continued up my special street, just a boy on his way home.

ACKNOWLEDGEMENTS

I spent years researching in the vast library of Holocaust literature to create *Primo*, settling on Auschwitz to depict the tragedy.

I am indebted to three exceptional authors whose autobiographies were instrumental in helping me understand and recreate the world of the concentration camps: Primo Levi: *Survival in Auschwitz* (1958), Elie Wiesel: *Night* (1960), and Tadeusz Borowski: *This Way for the Gas, Ladies and Gentlemen* (1959).

Each one touched me in a different way. Primo guided me with his insightful clarity that evoked a humanistic understanding of the tragedy. Elie brought the undertones of Jewish mysticism and spirituality that permeated Eastern European Judaism. Tadeusz, who was Polish, brought a defiant attitude, gutsy and daring, to his camp experience as he recreated that world so vividly, while defining its meaning so perceptively.

All of them were great writers in their own right, bearing witness to the evil they experienced, while illuminating the darkness of the human soul.